★ YOUR LUCK Is in the STARS

Jill M. Phillips

Publications International, Ltd.

Jill M. Phillips is the author of more than 300 published articles on astrology and related subjects, as well as over two dozen books, including the novels *The Rain Maiden* and *The Fate Weaver.* She regularly writes Forecast columns for *Astrology: Your Daily Horoscope* and contributes to *Globe*'s mini-magazine astrology series. Ms. Phillips works with clients through Moon Dancer AstroGraphics, her astrological counseling service.

ISBN: 0-7853-4531-0

CONTENTS

★ ★ ★ ★

INTRODUCTION

★ ★ ★ ★

WE LIVE IN a benevolent universe, where luck and good fortune abound. They are ours for the taking—if only we can learn to recognize just where these golden opportunities lie.

Are you lucky? Today? Tomorrow? In the future? Being open to good fortune begins with a state of mind. Positive people attract good luck.

In astrology, luck is signified by the presence of three planets: the Sun, Venus, and Jupiter. The Sun and Venus "visit" each sign for several weeks every year. A complete Jupiter cycle takes approximately 12 years, meaning that once every 12 years Jupiter transits (passes through) your sign, representing a period of significant good luck.

If you were born between July 23 and August 22, your Sun sign is Leo (see the Sun Sign Birth Chart on page 7). Thus, when the Sun transits Leo—from July 23 through August 22—you'll tend to be lucky. If you refer to the Venus transit table on page 92, you'll find that Venus will next transit Leo from August 26 to September 19, 2001—another lucky period for you.

Check out page 94 and discover the Jupiter transit table. It states that Lady Luck will visit Leos from August 1,

2002, through August 26, 2003—more than a full year of good fortune!

The 12 signs of the zodiac are subdivided into four "elements" symbolic of their general characteristics:

Fire signs: Aries, Leo, and Sagittarius. Those born under these signs are impetuous, passionate, and creative.

Earth signs: Taurus, Virgo, and Capricorn. Practical, thrifty, and wise.

Air signs: Gemini, Libra, and Aquarius. Witty, versatile, and sociable.

Water signs: Cancer, Scorpio, and Pisces. Intuitive, sensitive, and caring.

When the Sun, Venus, or Jupiter transit Leo, Leos can—as mentioned—expect good luck. Yet this also extends to the other two fire signs as well, since any planetary transit through Leo makes a favorable astrological aspect (called a "trine") to Aries and Sagittarius. When these planets transit an earth sign, all earth signs benefit. In order to see when these transits take place, see the tables at the back of the book.

Each sign of the zodiac has a planetary ruler whose energies are believed to shape the characteristics of that sign. If you are a Taurus or Libra (both ruled by Venus), a Leo (ruled by the Sun), or a Sagittarius (ruled by Jupiter), you may seem to be "born lucky." If so, you may possess a sixth sense about taking risks.

When the Sun is "in your sign" each year, the emphasis shifts to you, especially in personal matters. You feel focused, in touch with your feelings, able to make valuable and positive changes in your life.

Venus works its influence through resources, gifts, and the good will of friends, family members, and other loved ones. When Venus transits (or trines) your birth sign, you can expect good things to flow easily to you.

Jupiter's transit generally represents a period of major opportunities—financial windfalls, lucky alliances (such as marriage, friendship, or business partnerships), increased energy, and enthusiasm. You also have the optimistic attitude to take risks.

A word about retrograde phases: All planets, except for the Sun and Moon, have retrograde phases when they *appear* to be traveling in reverse. (They don't, of course, but the symbolism is the same.) These periods represent times when the planet's energies are less significant in our lives. In the case of Venus and Jupiter, a retrograde phase in your sign will generally signal a time when luck levels off. These are times when it is better not to take major risks or anticipate too great a financial return. You'll find the Jupiter retrograde table on page 95.

Sun Sign Birth Chart

★ ★ ★ ★

 Aries — March 21 - April 19

 Taurus — April 20 - May 20

 Gemini — May 21 - June 21

 Cancer — June 22 - July 22

 Leo — July 23 - August 22

 Virgo — August 23 - September 22

 Libra — September 23 - October 23

 Scorpio — October 24 - November 21

 Sagittarius — November 22 - December 21

 Capricorn — December 22 - January 19

 Aquarius — January 20 - February 18

Pisces — February 19 - March 20

ARIES

★ ★ ★ ★

Fire Sign

March 21 - April 19

YOUR SUN SIGN CHARACTERISTICS

ARIES ARE KNOWN for their straightforward, shoot-from-the-hip style. Fiercely independent, you speak your mind and seldom care if others agree with you.

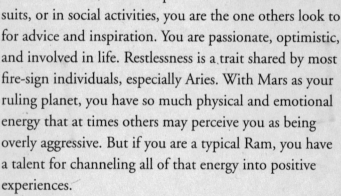

Aries individuals are natural leaders. At work, in leisure pursuits, or in social activities, you are the one others look to for advice and inspiration. You are passionate, optimistic, and involved in life. Restlessness is a trait shared by most fire-sign individuals, especially Aries. With Mars as your ruling planet, you have so much physical and emotional energy that at times others may perceive you as being overly aggressive. But if you are a typical Ram, you have a talent for channeling all of that energy into positive experiences.

You can be forceful and even argumentative at times. Anyone who knows you well realizes that you have a quick temper. In fact, it's safe to say that among family and friends you're probably known for it! But even though your temper flares up quickly, you cool down just as fast and almost never hold a grudge.

You love a challenge and may have a tendency to do things the hard way. If you have a choice between achieving a goal easily or taking the more difficult path to the same result, you will tend to choose the latter method.

Where appearance is concerned, Aries individuals have a great need to look their best at all times. Although you are always aware of the current trends, you understand that fashion is forever changing while style remains a constant factor. You have a style that is uniquely your own—classy, well-groomed, and striking. When you dress up, you feel better about yourself. Image is important to you, and you tend to judge others by the image they present.

YOUR LUCK: STRENGTHS AND WEAKNESSES

You are a risk-taker by nature, unafraid of the consequences that can result from making snap decisions or impulsive conclusions. As with most "extreme" attitudes, this trait can work both for and against you.

One of your best characteristics is an unfailing "can do" attitude and the ability to make things happen. You believe very strongly that people make their own good luck. The Aries approach to life seems to be: "There may be such a thing as luck in the universe, but it can't hurt to give it a little push."

As every Ram knows, belief in yourself helps you get what you want out of life. You are a courageous individual who can meet difficult or challenging times without losing faith in your own abilities.

One of the criticisms most often leveled at Aries is selfishness, or being too self-involved. It is true that the people of your sign are often egocentric, but as long as this doesn't blind you to the needs of others, it shouldn't be considered a negative characteristic. You simply need to be aware that your goals and ambitions aren't any more important than those of other people.

You don't always think before you speak, which can be a mistake. You excel at sarcasm, and you can be overly emotional at times.

YOUR LUCK IN: FAMILY

Despite your concentration on personal goals and projects, you always make plenty of time for family. Siblings, grown children, and grandchildren populate your personal landscape, bringing happiness and meaning to your life. Aries people are not "loner" types. For you, life is happiest when it is filled with the people you love.

Being involved in the lives of relatives keeps you feeling young, energized, and fulfilled. Because of the time and energy you put into your family life, you receive the same love and respect in return.

Whether they live close or at a distance, getting together with family members is most favorable when Venus transits Aries, Leo, or Sagittarius. (Transit: a planet's passage through a sign.) These transits are particularly good for making day excursions or taking short trips.

Jupiter's transit through the fire signs improves your relationships and can herald important family events, such as weddings and births. (See the Venus and Jupiter transit tables on pages 92–95.)

YOUR LUCK IN: RELATIONSHIPS

You are a "people person" with a wide circle of friends, associates, and even the occasional former love interest who has stayed around long enough to become a pal. Your friends play a major part in your life, and not just at social occasions. You share thoughts, feelings, and opinions with these people. They're family, by choice.

Venus, whose planetary influence governs relationships, also rules romantic love and possessions. Whenever Venus transits Aries, Leo, or Sagittarius, you can expect both romance and personal possessions to become important factors in your life.

Jupiter's transit through the fire signs brings new and interesting people into your circle. It also increases the occasions of generosity from friends, as well as opportunities to meet and socialize on a much grander scale.

YOUR LUCK IN: MONEY

Typical Aries natives are impulsive about everything, including money matters. This isn't to imply that you are reckless. The people of your sign seem to have an instinct about just how much to risk on anything from a department store purchase to a major financial investment.

Good luck is with you whenever Venus transits Aries, Leo, or Sagittarius, since the planet is responsible for bringing good things into your life with little or no effort on your part. These are also favorable times for gambling reasonable amounts of money at cards, at Bingo, or on sweepstakes tickets.

Jupiter's passage through Aries and the other fire signs generally accords with major periods of good fortune, especially in real estate or legal matters.

YOUR LUCK IN: HOME AND TRAVEL

Your home is your showplace, where you enjoy entertaining family members, friends, and associates. Venus transits in fire signs suggest favorable times for redecorating your home, while Jupiter transits promote good luck in buying or selling a home or any other real estate.

You love to travel, especially on package tours to large cities in the United States and Europe. Venus transits through Aries, Leo, and Sagittarius make for particularly good periods for traveling with friends and loved ones.

Beginning a trip during a favorable Venus transit makes the experience all the more enjoyable. Jupiter favors long-distance travel, travel for business purposes, or travel to meet legal or educational obligations.

YOUR LUCK IN: HEALTH AND SELF-IMPROVEMENT

You are the most energetic of all the 12 signs. Aries individuals can usually depend on vibrant good health throughout life, though there is a tendency to be accident-prone at times, especially when you are in a hurry. Exercise is vital to your well-being, since it helps you to channel your Mars energy in a positive direction.

When Venus transits Aries, Leo, and Sagittarius, you may have a tendency to put on weight because of cravings for sweets and other rich foods, though this can be controlled with proper exercise and diet. Jupiter's passage through the fire signs enhances your energy level and gives you a sense of spiritual and physical well-being.

LUCKY LISTS: ARIES

★ ★ ★ ★

YOUR LUCKY NUMBERS
1 • 5 • 10 • 20

YOUR LUCKY COLORS
Scarlet • White • Black • Tangerine

YOUR LUCKY STONES
Diamond • Ruby • Carnelian • Bloodstone

YOUR LUCKY DAY/MONTH
Sunday • April

YOUR LUCKY CITIES
San Francisco • Santa Barbara, CA • Portland, OR

YOUR LUCKY TRAVEL DESTINATIONS
England • Germany • Denmark

YOUR LUCKY PROFESSIONS
Politics • Medicine • Business

YOUR LUCKY HOBBIES
Swimming • Board Games • Volunteering

YOUR LUCKY ASSOCIATIONS (FRIENDS)
Leo • Libra • Sagittarius

MEDITATION
"There is no greater or more powerful force on earth than to believe in yourself."

TAURUS

★ ★ ★ ★

Earth Sign
April 20 - May 20

YOUR SUN SIGN CHARACTERISTICS

TAURUS INDIVIDUALS are beauty lovers with the ability to bring a sense of creativity to even the most mundane chores.

Because your sign is ruled by Venus, you have an inherent desire for peace and harmony. Yet when circumstances call for it, you can be scrappy and confrontational, proving that you deserve your sign's characterization as Taurus the Bull.

Taurus individuals are sensible, practical people who have a good sense of humor. You never seem to let your ego get in the way of relationships, and you can always manage to laugh at yourself when things get tough. Not taking yourself too seriously is one of your most endearing characteristics.

You have your feet planted firmly on the ground. You value the things in life that last, both material and spiritual. Change can be a real challenge for you since it seems to threaten everything that you hold dear: security, possessions, and tradition.

Taureans believe in pursuing a balanced approach to living. If you have put a lot of effort and energy into your family and other personal relationships, you understand the value of taking equal time for your own concerns. The same is true of career goals.

When it comes to style, Taureans remain conservative and traditional. You favor good grooming and quiet elegance. Outlandish or extreme fashions are simply not "you."

If you have a philosophy of life, it is probably this: "Live each day to the fullest. Take more pleasure in today than in thoughts of the past and dreams of the future."

YOUR LUCK: STRENGTHS AND WEAKNESSES

You probably get tired of being told how solid and dependable you are, but the fact is that these are your most positive personality traits. Add to that loyalty, common sense, and a warm nature and you've got a perfect description of the typical Taurean.

One of your best characteristics is a happy disposition. People feel better just being around you, and that is one of the reasons you have so many friends and are always in demand socially.

As every Bull knows, patience is a virtue. You have the ability to form far-reaching plans because of it. You don't expect to get all of your wishes granted at once. Working toward making your dreams come true helps you to appreciate them all the more.

On the negative side, you can be extremely stubborn at times. It may be hard for you to see things from someone else's point of view, and you aren't a bit shy about saying "I told you so" to a friend who has ignored your advice and come to regret it.

You don't lose your temper easily, but when you do, look out! Taureans are notorious for being slow to boil, but capable of rage when they've been pushed to the limits of their patience.

YOUR LUCK IN: FAMILY

The importance of family is a major factor in the life of Taureans. You have a somewhat old-fashioned concept of what family life should be that might be at odds with today's more liberated views. Yet that suits you just fine. You aren't about to change your values just to be "in fashion."

You believe in taking a real interest in the lives of family members. If you have grown children, you are seldom more than a phone call away. Grandchildren provide you with an opportunity to pass along the traditional values you hold dear. You're friendly with siblings. You get together for major holidays with them and are always supportive of their plans and projects.

Use Venus transits (transit: a planet's passage through a sign) to reconnect with relatives who live at a distance. Jupiter's passage through Taurus, Virgo, or Capricorn indicates periods when you can look forward to fortunate events in family life. (See the Venus and Jupiter transit tables on pages 92–95.)

YOUR LUCK IN: RELATIONSHIPS

You do some of your best work in the realm of relationships. With your natural talent for friendship, you don't have to worry about spending time alone. Although you are secure enough to be on your own, you prefer sharing things with the important people in your life.

When Venus transits your sign, there is always the chance that romantic love will come your way. The same is true when Venus is in Virgo and Capricorn. You have a healthy interest in the opposite sex and need a loving relationship in your life in order to feel whole.

Jupiter's passage through Taurus encourages you to expand your circle of friends, perhaps through association with a new club or group. This transit also increases the likelihood of a long-distance vacation. During these periods, legal matters are sure to go your way.

YOUR LUCK IN: MONEY

Taureans have a real flair for money; you know how to spend it and how to make it last. Best of all, you can budget on a shoestring and still manage to live like royalty. The only thing you refuse to do is take risks with your hard-earned cash. You're a T-bill and savings-account type of person, not a high-roller.

You like saving money in traditional ways, such as clipping coupons, mailing in rebates, and recycling. Possessions are important to you and represent your belief that hard work can bring you the things in life you want.

Venus transits in your sign improve your chances of making money through real estate. These are also favorable times to apply for a loan or invest in antiques. Jupiter's presence in Taurus and the other earth signs heralds good luck for wagering, especially in lottery tickets and Bingo.

YOUR LUCK IN: HOME AND TRAVEL

You are a homebody, and much of what you are as an individual can be found in the way you decorate and maintain your home. Whether it is grand or modest, your home is a showplace that represents how you feel about yourself and your accomplishments.

Entertaining at home is an important part of your social life and one of the things you do best. Venus transits in earth signs are favorable periods to decorate your home or hold an open house.

You like to travel in style. Venus transits promote good times to take trips with friends. Jupiter favors travel to distant places—the vacation you've dreamt about.

YOUR LUCK IN: HEALTH AND SELF-IMPROVEMENT

Your positive outlook on life does a lot to keep you feeling and looking good. Taureans do go for outlandish, rarefied beauty secrets. You believe in such things as eating food that is plain but tasty, limiting harmful practices such as smoking or consuming too much alcohol, and getting at least eight hours of sleep each night.

If you do have any health concerns, they are likely to be linked to food issues. The people of your sign often have a sweet tooth, and those rich, creamy desserts can be your downfall. Unfortunately, Venus and Jupiter transits can actually work against you when it comes to losing weight. Venus in your sign accentuates your desire for high-calorie foods, while Jupiter transits can mean expansion of your waistline.

Use the positive energy of these planetary transits to get involved in a new exercise program that will keep you fit. You are more likely to stick with a plan that allows you to feel good about your appearance while you are exercising, so dress appropriately but nicely.

LUCKY LISTS: TAURUS

★ ★ ★ ★

YOUR LUCKY NUMBERS
3 • 9 • 17 • 30

YOUR LUCKY COLORS
Pink • Peach • Beige • Lavender

YOUR LUCKY STONES
Emerald • Diamond • Rose Quartz • Lapis Lazuli

YOUR LUCKY DAY/MONTH
Thursday • May

YOUR LUCKY CITIES
Buffalo • El Paso • Honolulu

YOUR LUCKY TRAVEL DESTINATIONS
Ireland • Switzerland • Greek Islands

YOUR LUCKY PROFESSIONS
Interior Design • Banking • Music

YOUR LUCKY HOBBIES
Gardening • Needlepoint • Golf

YOUR LUCKY ASSOCIATIONS (FRIENDS)
Virgo • Scorpio • Capricorn

MEDITATION
"There is more power in an ounce of love than in a ton of hatred."

GEMINI

★ ★ ★ ★

Air Sign
May 21 - June 21

YOUR SUN SIGN CHARACTERISTICS

GEMINIS ARE WITTY with a powerful curiosity about life. You are known for having a way with words, and you've probably been invited to a great many dinners and parties based on your talent as a conversationalist.

And why not? With Mercury as your ruling planet, communication with others is the key to your nature. Not only is it important for you to express your own thoughts and ideas, but you are just as interested in learning about what others think.

Geminis can take any idea, put a lively spin on it, and turn it into something completely fascinating. Your intelligence is so rapid-fire that you can be a little intimidating at times. When people meet you, they are either put off or turned on by your need to exchange information. But no one can deny that your personality has an electric effect upon others.

You never grow tired of learning. That trait, combined with an upbeat, winning personality, can make you seem years younger than you actually are. You often surround yourself with young people because you enjoy the enthusiasm and optimism that they radiate.

While some people fear change, you embrace it. A need to be constantly challenged and intellectually engaged allows you to see the positive aspects in even the most difficult periods of transition.

Where appearance is concerned, you have a style all your own. Many Geminis have a tendency to dress younger than their age because it reflects how they feel about themselves. One thing is certain: On you, it works!

Your philosophy of life is based on a simple premise: If you can avoid getting bored, you will always be happy.

YOUR LUCK: STRENGTHS AND WEAKNESSES

Geminis are versatile and sociable. Because you always seem to be having such a good time, people love to be around you, and it's not uncommon for you to be the center of attention.

One of your best characteristics is your ability to handle more than one task or responsibility at a time. Whatever your age, you aren't intimidated by learning new skills or habits. That youthful approach to life keeps things interesting and insures that you never get bored.

You are extremely bright and possess a keen memory for facts and dates. Life is an adventure to you, a never-ending series of possibilities. Unlike many individuals, you aren't afraid to take risks in your personal or professional life. More than anything, Geminis believe in putting themselves "out there." No pain, no gain.

But like everyone, you also have your share of weak points. Because you enjoy conversation and the exchange of ideas and news, there is always a temptation to gossip, sometimes negatively, about people you know.

Your sharp wit can turn sarcastic at times, and you can be overly cynical. Unfortunately, procrastination is one of your worst traits. You don't mean to put things off, but you can't always seem to keep up with your own high expectations.

YOUR LUCK IN: FAMILY

At some point in your life—probably in your 20s or 30s—you may have experienced an emotional separation from your family. During those years, it was important for you to forge your own path, independent of family pressures. But now you have enough confidence to sustain good relationships with siblings and other family members. As a parent, you maintain a "pal" status with your children. You treat grown children as friends and equals, and they appreciate the sophisticated good humor you bring to this complicated relationship.

Venus transits through air signs (transit: a planet's passage through a sign) promote favorable relationships with sisters, daughters, and other female relatives. Jupiter transits bring periods of spiritual and material good fortune, as well as times when family members can come together in happiness and understanding. (See the Venus and Jupiter transit tables on pages 92–95.)

YOUR LUCK IN: RELATIONSHIPS

You aren't the kind of person who "screens" friends. As a rule, you like to surround yourself with a wide variety of acquaintances and pals, and it doesn't matter if they have a great deal in common with you or not. For Geminis, it is the differences that make a friendship interesting, challenging, and fun. You don't make judgments about friends; you support their choices, whatever your own feelings may be.

When it comes to romantic relationships, you are quite adventurous. Geminis are more likely than members of any other sign to get involved with a partner who is much younger or much older than themselves. Venus transiting Gemini, Libra, or Aquarius promotes an opportunity for a new romance. Jupiter in these signs revitalizes an existing relationship.

YOUR LUCK IN: MONEY

Geminis have a reputation for being spendthrifts who possess a casual attitude toward money. Actually, you have very good judgment when it comes to handling financial matters. Not exactly a risk-taker, you rely on intuition to help you make decisions about your finances. The fact that you don't have an emotional stake in how much money you earn or possess allows you to approach financial matters with analytical precision.

Venus transits encourage you to safeguard personal resources. These represent favorable times to increase the amount of insurance you carry and to initiate new savings plans. Spending money on your house is also a beneficial use of this transit.

Jupiter's passage through Gemini, Libra, or Aquarius represents major cycles of good luck. While you should not take any extreme risks, it is important to recognize financial opportunities as they appear.

YOUR LUCK IN: HOME AND TRAVEL

Travel is a part of your life. Busy Geminis are forever on the move, traveling for business, pleasure, or educational purposes. Communication is your key quality, and travel allows you to communicate with the ideas, the events, and the history all around you as nothing else can.

Despite your love for travel, you do treasure time spent at home. For you it represents a haven away from the world. Geminis have cultivated tastes and enjoy being surrounded by fine furnishings and tasteful decor.

When Venus transits through your sign, you might be inspired to buy new drapes, rugs, and furniture for your house. Also, search your attic or basement during these periods: Your "junk" could be worth a lot more than you realized! Jupiter promotes an interest in changing residences or improving the value of the property you already own.

YOUR LUCK IN: HEALTH AND SELF-IMPROVEMENT

Your ruling planet, Mercury, gives you a lot of nervous energy that can only be worked off through meditation and by pacing yourself. A hectic lifestyle makes you dependent on convenience, but eating on the run or eating too much fast food can negatively impact your health and fitness.

Your best bet for keeping fit is a brisk daily walk. Yoga promotes flexibility and relaxation. Caffeine is poison to high-strung Geminis, who need to supplement their diet with purified water and fresh-squeezed fruit and vegetable juices. You can also benefit from eating four or five small meals each day rather than three oversized ones.

Venus transits in Gemini and the other air signs promote high self-esteem and good body image. When Jupiter moves through these signs, you experience periods of increased emotional and physical energy.

LUCKY LISTS: GEMINI

★ ★ ★ ★

YOUR LUCKY NUMBERS
5 • 8 • 15 • 23

YOUR LUCKY COLORS
Yellow • Melon • Chartreuse • Cinnamon

YOUR LUCKY STONES
Agate • Alexandrite • Pearl • Cat's Eye

YOUR LUCKY DAY/MONTH
Wednesday • June

YOUR LUCKY CITIES
Hartford, CT • Houston • Las Vegas

YOUR LUCKY TRAVEL DESTINATIONS
Australia • Wales • Egypt

YOUR LUCKY PROFESSIONS
Journalism • Publishing • Teaching

YOUR LUCKY HOBBIES
Word Games • Skiing • Travel

YOUR LUCKY ASSOCIATIONS (FRIENDS)
Libra • Sagittarius • Aquarius

MEDITATION
"The only barrier to friendship is a closed mind."

CANCER

★ ★ ★ ★

Water Sign
June 22 - July 22

YOUR SUN SIGN CHARACTERISTICS

CANCERS ARE INTUITIVE with a talent for getting along with others. While you don't seek to impress those around you for superficial reasons, you are concerned with gaining their respect.

You are known for your ability to combine tenderness and tenacity, both in your relationships and your attitude toward life. Sensitive yet strong, you have very solid values that have helped to shape your character. While some of your ideas may strike others as slightly old-fashioned, you understand that the tried-and-true values have no expiration date.

Cancerians are extremely goal-oriented people. Once you set your mind on what you want to achieve, you will concentrate all of your efforts on making that dream come true. You can be incredibly single-minded, focusing all of your energy on a specific task. You are not afraid of hard work to bring a goal to fruition.

People who have seen only your soft side are amazed at your emotional toughness in the face of difficulties or disappointments. You are philosophical and able to roll with the punches. You adhere to the philosophy "when life gives you lemons, make lemonade." Though there are times when you may indulge in a "pity party," these are generally infrequent. Whenever you start feeling sorry for yourself, you count your blessings and end up feeling fortunate and thankful for all that you have.

With the Moon as your ruling planetary influence, you have a tendency to be moody. Because you are sensitive to the thoughts and feelings of others, your spirits may rise or fall based on how someone emotionally close to you is feeling.

Where appearance is concerned, Cancerians show their conservative nature. You don't like flashy or trendy styles or anything that makes it seem that you are trying to look like a teenager. You favor chic yet understated clothes and minimal accessories. While you accept the fact that most people judge on outer appearance, you also hope they will take the time to know the "inner" you.

YOUR LUCK: STRENGTHS AND WEAKNESSES

Everyone who knows you is inspired by your kind and nurturing persona. Helping people is what you do best, and you are always looking for ways to counsel and advise others.

Cancerians are natural care-givers. You pamper your loved ones, friends, and even professional colleagues, always ready to hear and sympathize with their problems. You are equally ready to be a cheerleader for their dreams and achievements.

Despite your natural sensitivity, you have a great deal of determination in your character. You are a hard worker and a good organizer. You don't give up easily, and you can always be counted on to come back even stronger after suffering a disappointment.

On the debit side, you sometimes have a problem letting go of negative experiences in your past. You have a long memory and may hold grudges against those who have wronged you.

Because you love so deeply, you have a tendency to "smother" the people you care about. You may feel sorry for yourself if others don't accord you the attention you feel you deserve, and you can become manipulative and emotionally clinging as a result. While you can be incredibly generous to others, there are times when you seek to control people with money or guilt.

YOUR LUCK IN: FAMILY

You have a respect for family that extends into every area of your life. You have an unconscious need to "mother" your relatives, even those who are your own age.

Cancer is the sign of "the mother," and whether or not you have children of your own, you will play this role through your relationships with other family members many times in your life. Because of your keen sensitivity, you may experience a psychic bond with close relatives, which allows you to feel that you can almost read their thoughts.

Venus transits through Cancer (transit: a planet's passage through a sign) promote happy family get-togethers and reunions. Jupiter's transit through Cancer and the other water signs is often a signifier of important family events. (See the Venus and Jupiter transit tables on pages 92–95.)

YOUR LUCK IN: RELATIONSHIPS

Cancerians know how to treat their friends. Close personal relationships form the center of your life, and you work very hard to keep those relationship fresh and interesting. In a romantic partnership, you are affectionate, caring, and loyal. If you are not currently in a relationship due to divorce or the death of a spouse, it can be difficult to get back into the dating scene again. Socializing with close friends can help you overcome your apprehensions.

When Venus, the planet of romantic love, transits your sign, you can expect romance to be a big part of your daily life. When Jupiter transits the water signs, it's a great time to establish new and fortunate relationships in your life.

YOUR LUCK IN: MONEY

Making money is important to you—for security reasons more than any other. You simply cannot feel safe unless you have money in the bank. Certainly you like to live well, but that is less of an issue than providing for your future in a way that makes you feel comfortable.

You aren't the risk-taking type. When it comes to safeguarding your finances, you are extremely conservative. You have a certain knack for making money by investing in real estate, but the numbers have to insure that you're going to make a profit before you'll commit to anything.

When Venus transits Cancer or the other water signs, you can expect the value of a possession to increase in value. Jupiter's transit could mean that a small legacy or bequest will come your way.

YOUR LUCK IN: HOME AND TRAVEL

For you, part of the attraction of travel is coming back to your own environment. That doesn't mean you don't enjoy trekking around the country or the world—you do. But by nature you are a home-loving individual whose happiest times are usually spent within the comfort of your own four walls. Your home reflects your need to retire into your "shell" when life outside gets too demanding and complicated. You like comfortable sur-roundings with an inviting decor—particularly in the kitchen, Cancer's favorite room.

When you travel, you often prefer cruises with your mate or a group of friends. Cancerians love to be on the water.

Choose Venus transits to plan redecorating or home remodeling chores. Jupiter transits in Cancer and other water signs are the best periods for long-distance travel.

YOUR LUCK IN: HEALTH AND SELF-IMPROVEMENT

More than those of any other sign, your physical health is tied to your emotions. If you're happy, you feel good. Similarly, any major problem in your life is certain to cause a blip on your health radar.

Many Cancerians have food issues that can be traced to emotional patterns set in childhood or adolescence. Keeping a food diary can help you understand your unconscious food triggers. Emphasizing good grooming and wearing flattering clothes promote a positive body image even if you are a few pounds overweight.

Venus transits allow you to focus on personal and self-improvement goals. When Jupiter moves through Can-cer, Scorpio, or Pisces, you can look forward to a boost in your energy level—a good time to rededicate yourself to a plan of daily exercise.

LUCKY LISTS: CANCER
★　★　★　★

YOUR LUCKY NUMBERS
2 • 6 • 12 • 26

YOUR LUCKY COLORS
Shell Pink • Forest Green • Silver • Vanilla

YOUR LUCKY STONES
Pearl • Moonstone • Ruby • Amber

YOUR LUCKY DAY/MONTH
Monday • June

YOUR LUCKY CITIES
Santa Fe • Oklahoma City • Richmond, VA

YOUR LUCKY TRAVEL DESTINATIONS
Holland • Scotland • New Zealand

YOUR LUCKY PROFESSIONS
Therapist • Home Economics • Investment Banker

YOUR LUCKY HOBBIES
Cooking • Power Walking • Genealogical Research

YOUR LUCKY ASSOCIATIONS (FRIENDS)
Pisces • Capricorn • Scorpio

MEDITATION
"Once gained, wisdom can never be lost."

LEO

★ ★ ★ ★

Fire Sign
July 23 - August 22

YOUR SUN SIGN CHARACTERISTICS

LEOS HAVE THE POWER to be leaders in all aspects of life. Your positive spirit and generous nature draw others to you with ease, and you willingly take on the mantle of leadership because it suits you so well.

You've got personality with a capital P. In fact, it's the dominant characteristic of your nature. Charm comes effortlessly to you. You couldn't keep your irrepressible personality under wraps even if you tried!

The people of your sign aren't likely to be found on the sidelines. In personal, professional, and even recreational areas of life, you plunge into the action, unafraid of the consequences. You would rather fail at something than be too timid to put yourself "out there."

Like other fire sign natives, you are renowned for having a quick temper. You are so emotional that it is impossible for you to keep your feelings to yourself. Drama comes easily to you, and while your reactions may seem "over the top," they are nevertheless your true feelings.

The Sun is your planetary influence and represents your generally sunny outlook on life. You aren't interested in looking at things from a negative perspective. If problems arise, you have what it takes to be critical. But for the most part, you believe that just about any difficulty can be handled by putting a positive spin on events. It is just that attitude that makes you such a great person to be around.

Personal appearance is a valuable part of your self-esteem. You have a true flair for fashion and are often seen as a trendsetter within your group. You always manage to look attractive by capitalizing on your best qualities and minimizing flaws. You favor a chic and somewhat flashy style that would overwhelm someone who doesn't possess your amazing presence. Accessories are a big part of your wardrobe and are likely to feature designer names.

YOUR LUCK: STRENGTHS AND WEAKNESSES

You are a friendly, sociable individual with a talent for being the life of the party. Your "people" skills are legendary, and you have a real talent for organization.

Leo is the sign of the Lion, and your vivacious personality certainly reflects that symbol. One of your greatest gifts is creativity, which may take many forms. Talents such as drawing, painting, writing, or perhaps even performing on stage or as a public speaker come easily to you.

One of your most endearing qualities is great personal courage, both physical and spiritual. You are never afraid to take a personal risk, especially when you understand that it is the only way to achieve a desired goal.

You are open-minded and somewhat blunt when it comes to expressing your opinions. Some may hold that against you, though most people appreciate your refreshing candor. Telling the truth is a way of life with you.

A typical criticism of Leos is that they are unable to admit when they are wrong. Ego is a very big issue with most people of your sign, and that can make it hard for you to admit mistakes. You also have a way of eclipsing others, since your own personality is excessively dynamic.

YOUR LUCK IN: FAMILY

Family life is a source of great joy and satisfaction for Leos. Your relationship with siblings, grown children, grandchildren, and even distant relatives is fueled by mutual love and respect as well as your interest in their lives and personal projects. While you are too independent to interfere in the lives of family members, you aren't above giving advice now and then.

Venus transits (transit: a planet's passage through a sign) encourage you to spend quality time with relatives, particularly female family members. These are also favorable periods to get to know new members of the family, such as in-laws. When Jupiter moves through the fire signs, you have a chance to act in an advisory role to a younger family member. (See the Venus and Jupiter transit tables on pages 92–95.)

YOUR LUCK IN: RELATIONSHIPS

You aren't the sort of person who enjoys going through life with only a few people at your side. Leos are gregarious, loving individuals who rejoice in having vital personal relationships and close friendships.

People like to be around you because you have a pleasant disposition that makes everyone in your circle feel better. A natural leader, you are the one friends turn to when they need advice, encouragement, or even a shoulder to cry on.

Whatever your age, romance continues to be an important part of your life. In order to be a complete and happy person, you need to have an engaging and rewarding love life.

Venus transits in Leo, Sagittarius, and Aries provide favorable times for you to get together with friends. Jupiter transits favor opportunities to get closer to old friends, and to make new ones.

YOUR LUCK IN: MONEY

When it comes to money, you always manage to see the big picture. You aren't reckless, but you appreciate the fact that in order to get a big return you sometimes have to gamble a little.

Leos have faultless good taste in everything, and that can cost a lot of money. But even if you live on a modest income, you manage to keep nice things around you. Entertaining friends is expensive, but it's an expense you are happy to incur. Nothing makes you happier than getting together with close friends in an upscale environment with you picking up the check.

Use Venus transits to look for bargains on expensive wardrobe items or furnishings. It is also a good time to buy lottery tickets or play other games of chance. Jupiter's passage through Leo, Sagittarius, and Aries signifies periods when your earning power is in the ascendant.

YOUR LUCK IN: HOME AND TRAVEL

Entertaining friends and business associates in your home is one of your favorite leisure pursuits. Like everything else about you, your home represents your personal style, charm, and good taste. You have a great deal of creative ability and are likely to take a hands-on interest in decorating your personal environment.

When you travel, you expect to have all the comforts of home at your fingertips. You love the romantic atmosphere of an Aegean cruise or a deluxe tour of the South of France.

Venus transits through the fire signs represent the most favorable periods to refurbish your home or take an extended vacation. Jupiter transits signify the luckiest times to buy or sell a house or other property.

YOUR LUCK IN: HEALTH AND SELF-IMPROVEMENT

Leos are active and energetic people with generally robust health. You don't believe in making health issues complicated. Eating sensibly and getting plenty of exercise keeps you in tip-top shape, but one of your "secrets" for feeling and looking good is your characteristic zest for life.

You are totally open to new ways and methods of improving your life. While you don't like fads, you do follow trends in health, fitness, and New Age matters. When you feel they can be beneficial, you incorporate them into your lifestyle.

Losing a bad habit is easiest when Venus transits your sign. When Jupiter moves through Leo, Sagittarius, or Aries, you have an opportunity to put long-range plans and goals into action.

LUCKY LISTS: LEO

★ ★ ★ ★

YOUR LUCKY NUMBERS
1 • 7 • 19 • 21

YOUR LUCKY COLORS
Gold • Hot Pink • Burnt Orange • Antique White

YOUR LUCKY STONES
Ruby • Sardonyx • Cinnabar • Citrine

YOUR LUCKY DAY/MONTH
Sunday • August

YOUR LUCKY CITIES
Baltimore • Boston • Chicago

YOUR LUCKY TRAVEL DESTINATIONS
Italy • France • Lebanon

YOUR LUCKY PROFESSIONS
Performing Arts • Public Speaking • Retail Sales

YOUR LUCKY HOBBIES
Drawing • Cycling • Entertaining

YOUR LUCKY ASSOCIATIONS (FRIENDS)
Sagittarius • Aquarius • Aries

MEDITATIONS
"Personal creativity is a form of liberation."

VIRGO

★ ★ ★ ★

Earth Sign

August 23 - September 22

YOUR SUN SIGN CHARACTERISTICS

VIRGOS ARE ANALYTICAL individuals who appreciate the nobility of service. Your common-sense approach to life is based on values that resonate deeply in your character. You are an advocate of fair play. As far as you're concerned, there is no such thing as a "free lunch."

Virgos are hard workers who refuse to take shortcuts when it comes to getting the job done. Whether you are the boss or just an employee, you will do your job well without asking yourself whether there is credit or praise to be won from the effort.

You not only believe in old-fashioned values, but you embrace them wholeheartedly. Still, that doesn't keep you from moving ahead with the times in other ways. With your gift for analytical problem-solving, computer skills come easily to you. Whatever your age, you see yourself as the consummate student, always excited about learning something new.

Mercury is your ruling planet, exerting a quixotic and sometimes unstable influence on you. Because of this, Virgos are known for being high-strung, excitable, and nervous at times. You are also a worrier, something that people who know you come to accept as part of your personality.

Because of your basically shy and retiring nature, it can be hard for others to get to know you. Your dignified persona can even be a little off-putting to some. But when people look beyond the image that you project, they see a warm and giving person who strives hard to do the right thing. One of your best traits is a sense of humor that can even be a little naughty at times. You love to shock people with your jokes and observations.

Where appearance is concerned, Virgos cultivate a discreet elegance. You aren't interested in being a slave to fashion, preferring to showcase your quiet, discerning persona through timeless fashions.

YOUR LUCK: STRENGTHS AND WEAKNESSES

No one understands the phrase "God is in the details" like Virgos. Your talent for handling such things signifies a fine, orderly mentality. Virgos are intelligent, bookish types who possess a wry sense of humor. You are a practical earth sign, but that doesn't keep you from being able to see the funny side of things.

Virgos are the most dependable people on the planet. When you make a promise to someone, you are sure to follow through. One of your most engaging characteristics is loyalty. You will stand by a friend or loved one no matter what. When it comes to those you care for, you can always manage to refrain from being judgmental.

Despite your many good points, you aren't perfect. Virgos are extremely critical, and your fault-finding can be exasperating to others. Also, though your attention to detail is laudable, it can keep you from seeing the "big picture." Moreover, your critical nature can keep you from seeing things from a positive point of view. You can be sarcastic at times, especially if you are feeling insecure.

YOUR LUCK IN: FAMILY

You have tremendous respect for the traditions of family life and the emotional warmth created by a close family circle. As a traditionalist, you may be uncomfortable with the attitudes of the younger generation that do not conform to your own way of thinking. But despite any differences, you are always able to maintain close and meaningful ties with those you love.

Virgos are not particularly good at showing their innermost feelings, even to their closest family members.

Venus transits through Virgo (transit: a planet's passage through a sign) create an atmosphere that allows you to let down your guard to family members and show your affection in a more demonstrative way.

Jupiter transits accord with the rise of good fortune in family life, both material and spiritual. (See the Venus and Jupiter transit tables on pages 92–95.)

YOUR LUCK IN: RELATIONSHIPS

You may not have a large circle of friends, but you treat those you do have like family. You probably have some friends who have been with you for many years, since you aren't the type to change friends when your lifestyle or personal circumstances undergoes a change.

Venus is the planet that rules all types of relationships, including romantic ones. When Venus transits Virgo, Capricorn, or Taurus, you are more inclined to begin a romantic adventure. Or, in the case of an existing union, the relationship will be revitalized and refreshed.

Under the influence of a Jupiter transit, you can expect to begin interesting friendships with people who share your ideals and who can bring good fortune into your life.

YOUR LUCK IN: MONEY

Few people are as competent as you at handling money. You are extremely practical and have the discipline necessary to live within a budget. While you have a taste for the nicer things in life, you are not willing to go into debt in order to own them.

Like all earth signs, you have an appreciation for material things, but that doesn't mean you are materialistic. You have an eye for value and are not the type to throw good money after bad. Many Virgos are shrewd investors, but only if the downside isn't too steep.

When Venus transits Virgo, Capricorn, or Taurus, you can expect resources to come your way with little or no effort on your part. This is a good time to apply for a loan, refinance property, or increase your savings. Jupiter cycles are extremely fortunate for earth signs, indicating a possible legacy or windfall.

YOUR LUCK IN: HOME AND TRAVEL

Virgos keep a tidy, well-ordered home. To you, it doesn't matter if your residence is modest or mansion-sized. You believe in a place for everything and everything in its place.

Venus transits in earth signs indicate favorable periods to dress up your home, or to make investments in real estate. Jupiter transits signal appropriate times to look for and find your "dream house."

You like to travel, but because of a nervous nature, you don't travel well. You prefer short jaunts and getaways to long-distance travel. It is lucky to start a trip or vacation when Venus is transiting Virgo, Capricorn, or Taurus. When Jupiter moves through these signs, you could find yourself traveling for business or educational purposes. This can also signify a visit to you by a foreign friend.

YOUR LUCK IN: HEALTH AND SELF-IMPROVEMENT

Virgo is the sign of health consciousness, which means that you probably have very good nutritional and fitness habits. Virgos often become vegetarians or vegans, and you are more likely than other signs to be aware of the effects of what you are putting into your body.

Mercury is your planetary ruler, so you have a tendency to be high-strung, with a lot of nervous energy to spare. Caffeine and nicotine are very harmful to your sensitive body chemistry, and stress is your worst enemy. Exercise, especially something that involves a mind/body synergy such as yoga, helps you to handle stress in a positive way.

Personal self-improvement is favored whenever Venus transits Virgo. When Jupiter transits any of the earth signs, you can expect your energy to be at its peak.

LUCKY LISTS: VIRGO

★ ★ ★ ★

YOUR LUCKY NUMBERS
6 • 14 • 22 • 34

YOUR LUCKY COLORS
Midnight Blue • Mango • Sable • Cranberry

YOUR LUCKY STONES
Periodot • Sapphire • Beryl • Jade

YOUR LUCKY DAY/MONTH
Wednesday • September

YOUR LUCKY CITIES
Los Angeles • Colorado Springs • Reading, PA

YOUR LUCKY TRAVEL DESTINATIONS
West Indies • Crete • Brazil

YOUR LUCKY PROFESSIONS
Communications • Accounting • Real Estate

YOUR LUCKY HOBBIES
Sewing • Yoga • Poetry

YOUR LUCKY ASSOCIATIONS (FRIENDS)
Capricorn • Pisces • Taurus

MEDITATION
"Positive thoughts have a life all their own."

LIBRA

* * * *

Air Sign
September 23 - October 23

YOUR SUN SIGN CHARACTERISTICS

LIBRAS ARE CHARMING individuals with a talent for saying the right thing at the right time. You are known for your elegance, affability, and artistic sensibilities. Libras are very sociable with a reputation for enjoying the high life. You like people and being part of a large social circle. You like to feel involved, included, a part of the action.

Venus is your ruiing planet, making beauty and romance a major factor in your life. You have a positive, youthful attitude, and because of that you may seem much younger than your actual age.

Libras are fair, just, and reasonable people who do everything possible to live in harmony with others. Not only do you dislike arguments and discord, but such things can actually make you ill. Despite this sensitivity, you are an extremely strong and determined individual. You are ambitious, too, though this is a side of you that many people don't see.

You may seem to be all "sugar and spice," but there is an iron will behind that pleasant persona. The major difference between you and most people is that you are incredibly discreet about your personal motivations. Libras always like to hold a little of themselves in reserve, keeping people "guessing."

When it comes to looking good, Libras wrote the book. You're stylish and attractive and work very hard to keep yourself that way. You have an innate flair for color and style, always able to choose just the right look.

You have an instinct for what trends work for you and which ones don't. When you were very young, you probably worried about staying slim enough to look fashionable. Now you understand that true beauty radiates from within.

YOUR LUCK: STRENGTHS AND WEAKNESSES

Libra is the most highly praised of the 12 zodiacal signs. All your life you have been reading magazine articles and astrology books that describe your charm, sweetness, and good looks.

Guess what? They were right! Libras possess all those traits, and more. Maybe it's because you strive so hard to achieve balance, which is your personality keynote. In trying to find that spiritual and emotional equilibrium, you tap into many wonderful characteristics and strengths.

One of your best traits is composure in the face of any problem. It's that same grace that allows you to be the peacemaker when friends or family members argue.

Libras have a sweet temperament, but that doesn't mean you can't be steely and resolute when the situation warrants it. Think of it as your "secret weapon." With your pleasant disposition and winning personality, no one would ever think you were capable of so much as a frown.

On the debit side, you have a fear of confrontation and worry too much about whether or not people like you. This can create a lack of honesty in your relationships, causing you to care more about superficial appearances than the truth. Sometimes you have trouble making a decision, constantly vacillating between two points of view, which can be aggravating to those around you.

YOUR LUCK IN: FAMILY

Although you are caring and affectionate, you don't like to interfere in the lives of family members. It's enough for you to keep in touch, cheering quietly from the sidelines as grown children, siblings, and other relatives achieve their goals. But you don't expect them to look after you, and you don't encourage them to come to you for advice.

This is one of the ways in which you display your need for independence. As compatible as you are with those you love, you don't like the idea of leaning on others for emotional support.

Venus transits through air signs (transit: a planet's passage through a sign) indicate favorable periods to get together with family members. Jupiter's passage in these signs represents emotional high points in your relationships with relatives. (See the Venus and Jupiter transit tables on pages 92–95.)

YOUR LUCK IN: RELATIONSHIPS

No one is more devoted to making relationships work than Libras. Whether it is romance, friendship, or a professional partnership, you understand that in order to get along, the parties involved must treat each other with kindness and respect. One of the reasons you have such a profound understanding of "togetherness" is because Venus, which governs all relationships, rules your sign.

When it comes to romance, you are extremely idealistic, meaning you sometimes make unwise choices. But you know that love can't be measured strictly by the things two people have in common. Whenever Venus transits Libra, you are concerned with the romantic aspects of a love relationship. Venus in Aquarius or Gemini allows you to meet new people and pursue new friendships.

Jupiter transits create an atmosphere of joy and excitement. During these cycles, you are drawn to people who share your ideals and values.

YOUR LUCK IN: MONEY

Money is not a status symbol to you, just a means by which you can buy the expensive and beautiful things you love. Libras love to shop—for clothes, accessories, furnishings, the works! Yet despite this desire to live well, you don't make material things the center of your life.

Venus transits in Libra, Aquarius, and Gemini make you more aware of the importance you place on surrounding yourself with lovely things. They also indicate periods when your resources—home, antiques, art—are likely to increase in value.

When Jupiter moves through Libra and the other air signs, you can expect existing investments to pay more than usual, though new investments should be kept to a minimum at this time.

YOUR LUCK IN: HOME AND TRAVEL

Whether at home or on the road, you enjoy being surrounded by beautiful things. You aren't the type who likes to live life on the economy plan. Tasteful and harmonious settings have a major effect on your physical and emotional well-being. You simply cannot be happy in an environment without charm and at least a few luxuries.

When you travel, you like visiting America's big cities or sophisticated European capitals, which offer the best life has to offer in shopping, dining, and the arts.

Venus transits in Libra promote an interest in redecorating your home or taking a cruise with a lover or group of friends. When Jupiter moves through Libra, Aquarius, or Gemini, you can expect to have the financial wherewithal to relocate, perhaps to a foreign city.

YOUR LUCK IN: HEALTH AND SELF-IMPROVEMENT

Libras seem to radiate a glow of happiness and good health, even though they aren't sticklers about taking care of themselves. You like to look good, which is about the only thing that can convince you to exercise. Delightful though they are, Libras are known for being somewhat lazy.

With Venus as your planetary ruler, it's likely that you often crave rich foods—especially desserts. Cutting back on calories can be difficult for you, particularly if you sometimes find yourself eating for emotional rather than nutritional reasons.

While the presence of Venus in Libra or the other air signs can trigger cravings, you can also use its influence to enforce good habits and discard bad ones. Jupiter transits give you a boost of energy and a sense of emotional and physical well-being.

LUCKY LISTS: LIBRA

★ ★ ★ ★

YOUR LUCKY NUMBERS
7 • 12 • 21 • 27

YOUR LUCKY COLORS
Lilac • Baby Blue • Jade Green • Fuchsia

YOUR LUCKY STONES
Opal • Jasper • Rose Quartz • Blue Lace Agate

YOUR LUCKY DAY/MONTH
Thursday • October

YOUR LUCKY CITIES
Roswell, NM • Knoxville, TN • Eugene, OR

YOUR LUCKY TRAVEL DESTINATIONS
Austria • Japan • Tibet

YOUR LUCKY PROFESSIONS
Fashion • Law • Catering

YOUR LUCKY HOBBIES
Shopping • Jazzercise • Movies

YOUR LUCKY ASSOCIATIONS (FRIENDS)
Aquarius • Aries • Gemini

MEDITATION
"Only by letting go of the past will you be free to celebrate your future."

SCORPIO

★ ★ ★ ★

Water Sign

October 24 - November 21

YOUR SUN SIGN CHARACTERISTICS

SCORPIOS ARE INTENSE individuals with a talent for keeping secrets. You are known for your determined nature and strong purpose of will.

Scorpios are very emotional individuals, but they are not always comfortable sharing these emotions with others. They even keep those they love at arm's length. It is often said that Scorpios enjoy prying into other people's secrets but never give away any of their own.

You are impervious to criticism and will never change your own personality traits in order to please other people. They either accept you as you are or not at all.

Pluto is your planetary ruler, and its influence gives you the talent for profound inner transformation. Power is the keynote of your nature, but you know that for it to be a completely positive experience in your life, you must use it with care and discretion. Scorpios automatically sense the power dynamics of their relationship with others and often seek to tilt the balance in their favor.

One of your premier characteristics is tenacity. When you get involved in a project, you put your whole heart and soul into it. As you see it, anything worth attempting deserves your total concentration and focus.

You have the potential to be a leader, but you may prefer to operate from behind the scenes rather than in an up-front capacity. So long as you can wield the power and influence, you don't care if you get the credit. You have a healthy ego, but you don't require the external validation of others.

Where appearance is concerned, you have very definite ideas. It doesn't matter what everybody else is wearing; you feel the need to express your iconoclastic nature through the way you dress. You aren't really concerned with your looks, because you manage to feel good about yourself regardless of whether you are dressed to the nines or wearing jeans. Scorpios look good in black, with few accessories.

YOUR LUCK: STRENGTHS AND WEAKNESSES

Your best and worst trait is the same: You are a person of great extremes. There doesn't seem to be any middle ground for you.

On the positive side, you are loyal, determined, and virtually fearless. You have strong opinions about nearly everything, and you have the courage of your convictions to stand up for what you believe, however controversial it may be.

One of your best traits is your endurance, both physical and emotional. You can work at a job or task for many hours without getting bored or tired.

There is absolutely nothing fake or shallow about you. Scorpios are the real article. You couldn't care less if your remarks or opinions offend someone. You speak the truth as you see it, and if others don't like it, too bad!

You couldn't care less about fads or trends; Scorpios set their own trends. Nor do you try to make people like you. They either do or they don't. Either way, it doesn't bother you.

Jealousy is your worst trait. If you are unable to control that aspect of your personality, it can have a very negative effect on your life. You are also known for holding grudges against those you feel have done you wrong. Your emotions are strong, and when you love someone you almost seem to absorb their personality into your own.

YOUR LUCK IN: FAMILY

Your loyalty finds a perfect outlet in family life. No matter how much you may disagree with members of your family, you will always back them up. You make it known that you expect the same treatment.

Although you revere family life and all the traditions it represents, these issues can be complex for you at times. Your involvement with grown children and siblings is often complicated by your intense need to be the dominant force in these relationships.

When Venus transits through water signs (transit: a planet's passage through a sign), some of the tension inherent in family matters is relaxed. During such times, you are better able to confide in a relative. Jupiter transits have the power to improve a family issue that may have been troublesome in the past. (See the Venus and Jupiter transit tables on pages 92–95.)

YOUR LUCK IN: RELATIONSHIPS

You are a loner by preference, yet relationships have a profound influence on your life. More than any other sign, you understand the extraordinary dynamics at work in a union between two people.

Because you aren't the social type, your circle of friends is likely to be small but intense. Friends are more than just "pals" to you; they are practically family.

In romantic relationships, you give everything you have, looking to achieve a spiritual as well as physical partnership. You believe in a union that is meaningful.

Venus transits through your sign enhance romance and could correspond with an exciting new love relationship. The presence of Jupiter gives you the optimism you need to bring new people into your sphere.

YOUR LUCK IN: MONEY

Money is a power issue with you and has the potential to impact your relationships. Although you don't measure your accomplishments by how much money you have, your sense of security is inevitably tied to your financial position.

You have a great respect for money, which keeps you from spending it foolishly. When it comes to investing, you favor the conservative approach. You would rather get a smaller return from a regular savings account than tie up savings in a risky investment.

However, when Venus moves through Scorpio, Pisces, or Cancer, you can expect small wagers or risks to be fortunate for you. A Jupiter transit is even more lucky and could signal a pay raise.

YOUR LUCK IN: HOME AND TRAVEL

Your home is a haven from the outside world, a place to escape the pressures of daily life. You prefer comfortable, even homey surroundings, where you can feel at ease and let your hair down.

Travel adventures are often pilgrimages for Scorpios. You take vacations to learn and experience something special. Unlike other signs, you don't mind traveling alone. In fact, you sometimes prefer the opportunity to dwell on your own impressions and observations.

Travel, especially sea voyages with a romantic partner, is enhanced when Venus passes through your sign. When Jupiter transits Scorpio, Pisces, or Cancer, you are likely to seek out a place of great spiritual significance.

YOUR LUCK IN: HEALTH AND SELF-IMPROVEMENT

Because you have a strong constitution and a great potential for endurance, you probably don't have to do a lot to keep healthy. Like most things, your attitude toward fitness runs to extremes. You may ignore the conventional wisdom about nutrition and yet never gain a pound. Or you may be largely sedentary and still be incredibly fit. It's hard for you to conform to complicated ideas about health, since you like to keep things simple. When it comes to breaking bad habits, you prefer to do it without any professional help.

Venus transits are excellent periods to concentrate on making lifestyle changes since you are generally in a happier, more relaxed frame of mind at such times. Jupiter represents the most favorable time to begin a diet or new exercise plan, because besides boosting your energy level, the transit gives you an "I can" attitude.

LUCKY LISTS: SCORPIO

★ ★ ★ ★

YOUR LUCKY NUMBERS
2 • 11 • 24 • 32

YOUR LUCKY COLORS
Cherry Red • Mauve • Evergreen • Royal Blue

YOUR LUCKY STONES
Topaz • Tourmaline • Jet • Onyx

YOUR LUCKY DAY/MONTH
Friday • November

YOUR LUCKY CITIES
Denver • Little Rock • Philadelphia

YOUR LUCKY TRAVEL DESTINATIONS
Norway • Korea • Morocco

YOUR LUCKY PROFESSIONS
Scientific Research • Insurance • Healing

YOUR LUCKY HOBBIES
Self-Improvement • Racquetball • Occult Research

YOUR LUCKY ASSOCIATIONS (FRIENDS)
Pisces • Taurus • Cancer

MEDITATION
"The greatest success comes from maintaining your ideals."

SAGITTARIUS

★ ★ ★ ★

Fire Sign
November 22 - December 21

YOUR SUN SIGN CHARACTERISTICS

SAGITTARIANS ARE ADVENTUROUS individuals who gain wisdom through experience. You are known for your intelligence, wit, and love of people. While not necessarily sociable in the traditional sense, you have a talent for being both independent and happy as part of a group.

The people of your sign are enthusiastic individuals who always manage to see things from a positive point of view. You definitely believe that the proverbial glass is half full, not half empty. Even when disappointments come your way, nothing can keep you down for long.

Sagittarians are the truth-tellers of the zodiac. Even if a piece of personal information reflects badly on you, you aren't shy about sharing it. As far as you are concerned, total honesty is the key to happiness.

Jupiter, known as the "Greater Benefic," is your planetary ruler, making you extremely generous in the way you treat yourself as well as others. That is one of the reasons you don't like details and have such disdain for people who are cheap. To you, life is a never-ending party, and you are the guest of honor.

Of course, you have your serious side, too. Sagittarians have a reputation for being extremely smart, though your knowledge isn't limited to book learning alone. You believe that in order to learn about life, you need to roll up your sleeves and get real hands-on experience.

One of your most endearing characteristics is your tolerance for the opinions of others. Whether the subject is politics, religion, the arts, or sports, you enjoy having a lively discussion with people whose views differ from your own.

Where style is concerned, Sagittarians generally favor comfort over fashion. Naturally you like to look nice, but to you that is synonymous with "casual." Keeping up with current trends and styles is fun for you, as long as the "rules" aren't restrictive.

YOUR LUCK: STRENGTHS AND WEAKNESSES

Sagittarians have a sunny, positive outlook on life. You also have an adventurous streak that sets you apart from others. To you, life is a long journey filled with challenges, surprises, and maybe a few heartaches. But so long as you keep interested and involved, you're happy.

You have a youthful personality that enchants everyone who knows you. Because Sagittarius is the sign of higher education, learning is important to you. You are a student of life, always fascinated with developing new interests and learning about new subjects.

One of the frequent criticisms leveled at Sagittarians is that they speak without thinking. They can be blunt to the point of rudeness. You don't mean to be unkind or critical, but your unsolicited comments often come at the wrong time. Despite your warm and friendly nature, you sometimes have trouble with intimacy issues, and you may keep people at a distance.

One of your best traits is also one of your worst. Optimism is a way of life for Sagittarians, but it can be taken to extremes, especially when wagering. Your love of gambling can become an obsession.

YOUR LUCK IN: FAMILY

Despite your love of independence and need to stand on your own, you are firmly committed to being a part of family life. Sagittarians love big, extended families, especially those that embrace several generations. You always feel that you can learn from those older and younger than yourself.

Because you are so young at heart, you have a special connection with grandchildren. Yet, no matter how devoted you are to the younger generation, you aren't the type to meddle or be demanding.

Venus transits in fire signs (transit: a planet's passage through a sign) promote happy get-togethers with family members, especially sisters, daughters, and granddaughters. Jupiter cycles usually indicate that something wonderful is about to happen in your family life, perhaps a wedding or the birth of a child. (See the Venus and Jupiter transit tables on pages 92–95.)

YOUR LUCK IN: RELATIONSHIPS

You are a warm person who enjoys surrounding yourself with lots of good friends. Even though you are emotionally equipped to spend time on your own, you like the feeling of celebration that comes only when you are in the company of others. Friends are an integral part of your existence, almost like family.

Sagittarians are romantic, yet shy of commitment. You like to know that you are in command of your life, not following in the footsteps of a spouse or lover. Sagittarians are able to maintain friendships with the opposite sex, or with a former spouse or partner.

Expect friends to be especially generous and helpful when Venus transits Sagittarius, Aries, or Leo. When Jupiter transits these sectors, you are likely to begin a new and positive relationship.

YOUR LUCK IN: MONEY

Easy come, easy go. That's a Sagittarian's reputation with money. It's not that you are foolish about the way you handle it, but your generosity is legendary.

Sagittarians spend money freely, always optimistic that there is more where that came from. That isn't simply a frivolous attitude on your part, but a form of positive thinking that is akin to "outflow." You believe that spending money is a more positive act than saving it. However, it is important that you distinguish between being open-handed and being generous to a fault.

Nearly every Sagittarian has a weakness for gambling. This is a harmless hobby so long as you don't wager more than you can afford to lose.

Venus transits bring good luck through increased earnings and improved resources. When Jupiter—your lucky planet—moves through the fire signs, you have a better chance of winning at the lottery and other forms of gaming.

YOUR LUCK IN: HOME AND TRAVEL

Travel is a way of life for most Sagittarians. As much as you love your home, you never lose your taste for visiting exciting places. It doesn't have to be anywhere exotic or unusual; Sagittarians can get as much entertainment from a weekend getaway as some individuals can from a

Caribbean cruise. At home, you foster an open, happy environment where friends, family members, and even business associates feel welcome to drop by at any time.

When Venus is transiting Sagittarius, Aries, or Leo, you should make plans for extended travel. Jupiter in these signs represents good periods to buy or sell a house or even relocate to another city.

YOUR LUCK IN: HEALTH AND SELF-IMPROVEMENT

Natural enthusiasm and zest for life are reasons that Sagittarians generally enjoy such good health. Another reason is your love of exercise. Sports have probably played an important part in your life, and you have no difficulty adhering to a disciplined exercise routine on a regular schedule. Best of all, since you remain involved in the mainstream of life, you feel fit, both physically and spiritually.

Use the positive energy of Venus transits in the fire signs to begin a new health regimen. Jupiter transits will give you the optimism and drive you need to get rid of bad habits and incorporate good ones into your life.

LUCKY LISTS: SAGITTARIUS

★ ★ ★ ★

YOUR LUCKY NUMBERS
4 • 16 • 25 • 31

YOUR LUCKY COLORS
Royal Purple • Turquoise • Cream • Navy Blue

YOUR LUCKY STONES
Blue Quartz • Zircon • Azurite • Turquoise

YOUR LUCKY DAY/MONTH
Tuesday • December

YOUR LUCKY CITIES
Cheyenne • Spokane, WA • Anchorage

YOUR LUCKY TRAVEL DESTINATIONS
Spain • South Africa • Canada

YOUR LUCKY PROFESSIONS
Marriage Counselor • Travel Agent • Editor

YOUR LUCKY HOBBIES
Languages • Snow Sports • Writing

YOUR LUCKY ASSOCIATIONS (FRIENDS)
Aries • Gemini • Leo

MEDITATION
"Finding a way to serve others reflects the beauty
of your soul."

CAPRICORN

★ ★ ★ ★

Earth Sign
December 22 - January 19

YOUR SUN SIGN CHARACTERISTICS

CAPRICORNS ARE AMBITIOUS individuals who succeed in life. You are extremely disciplined and have the ability to act as a mentor and inspiration to others.

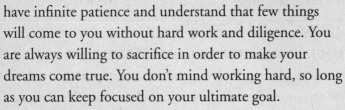

The keynote to your personality is caution and control. You have infinite patience and understand that few things will come to you without hard work and diligence. You are always willing to sacrifice in order to make your dreams come true. You don't mind working hard, so long as you can keep focused on your ultimate goal.

As a Capricorn, you know what you want out of life. Even if you must take a circuitous route to get there, get there you will! Saturn is your ruling planet, giving you the tenacity and common sense to focus on demanding long-range plans. You are also detail-oriented. By combining these talents, you are usually able to formulate plans that are both ambitious and within your reach.

Although you can't really be described as a "people person," you have a great talent for dealing with individuals from all walks of life. Your innate sense of honesty and fair play allows you to be in charge without seeming bossy or intrusive.

You care about your reputation and work hard at maintaining it. Your sense of caution comes into play when you must make a decision that may require you to compromise your strong sense of ethics.

Style plays an important part in your life. You like to look good and dress well, but you're adverse to flashiness or other "looks" that are inappropriate for you. Capricorns have a rare instinct for being tasteful. Expensive materials and elegant accessories keep you looking chic and elegant on all occasions.

YOUR LUCK: STRENGTHS AND WEAKNESSES

Capricorns are practical, sensible, and responsible individuals. Sound boring? Not at all! Those are the characteristics that the world sees, but people who know you best realize that you are much more. You have a wicked sense of fun, and your sense of humor can be extremely self-deprecating at times.

You aren't the sort who is comfortable with change, but you know better than to resist it. Saturn makes you cautious, but it also gives you wisdom. If you can learn from a difficult situation—and you generally do—you consider it more of a blessing than a problem.

One of your best traits is intelligence. Although you respect education, you know that some things can only be learned through experience. While you are dedicated to getting ahead in life, you also believe in playing by the rules. Capricorns are good citizens who respect law and authority.

Like everyone, you also have your negative traits. Despite your efforts to appear very self-controlled and confident, you may actually feel insecure and self-conscious a great deal of the time, particularly in social situations. Because status means so much to you, you tend to think that everyone is judging you. Sometimes, you deliberately form friendships that can help you in personal or professional circumstances.

YOUR LUCK IN: FAMILY

With your talent for leadership, you are probably the driving force behind your family group. Loyalty is your middle name, and you can always be counted on to help a family member who needs emotional support, advice, or even a loan.

Childless Capricorns are famous for treating nieces and nephews like their own children. If you do have kids, you probably can't wait to be a grandparent. Capricorns are known as strict parents but relax their rules with grandchildren.

Venus transits (transit: a planet's passage through a sign) have a heartwarming effect on your relationship with close family members. When Jupiter moves through Capricorn, Taurus, or Virgo, you are likely to be drawn into the financial circumstances of a relative, generally for the better. (See the Venus and Jupiter transit tables on pages 92–95.)

YOUR LUCK IN: RELATIONSHIPS

You keep a tight rein on your emotions, but those who matter most in your life know who they are. You are quite selective when it comes to choosing friends and often surround yourself with pals who share your professional or social standing. You're not a snob, but you do feel more comfortable with people who are very much like you. Capricorns are very discreet when it comes to romantic matters. If a relationship breaks up, you do all you can to make sure that the parting is amicable.

A new relationship—either romantic or platonic—is likely to come your way when Venus transits your sign. Jupiter's passage through Capricorn and the other earth signs usually suggests an improvement in the resources of a close associate—or you may use your own good fortune to help a friend in need.

YOUR LUCK IN: MONEY

No one handles finances as well as Capricorns. You have an enormous respect for money, which makes you conservative with finances. Living well is important to you, but you are more intent on building up financial security through savings and solid investments.

Although you don't mean to be tight with a buck, it can be hard for you to be as open-handed with money as you would like. This is part of a "scarcity mentality" that is often associated with practical earth signs. Though you may not want to change your attitudes toward money, you could actually improve your chances of acquiring more wealth if you became less rigid.

Use Venus transits to make small but worthwhile inroads into "outflow mentality." By giving to charity, helping out a friend, or simply spending money on yourself, you are encouraging providence to reward your generosity. When Jupiter transits the earth signs, good luck comes your way effortlessly. During these cycles, real estate, jewelry, and antiques make excellent investments.

YOUR LUCK IN: HOME AND TRAVEL

You see your home as a reflection of your own good taste. Entertaining friends and associates in this setting makes you feel good about yourself and what you have been able to achieve in life. Capricorns are knowledgeable collectors, and your home is likely to be filled with fine furniture, attractive art, and plenty of interesting knickknacks.

You like to travel, but only on your own terms. That means first class all the way, and with a budget that allows you to stay in the best hotels and eat in the finest restaurants. You have the ability to "rough it" if necessary, but that's not something you enjoy.

Venus transits give you the inspiration to buy new and attractive items for your home—often at bargain prices. Plan a major trip or vacation whenever Jupiter transits Capricorn, Taurus, or Virgo.

YOUR LUCK IN: HEALTH AND SELF-IMPROVEMENT

You have the discipline to maintain sensible health and fitness habits. You know the value of good nutrition, exercise, and getting plenty of rest. Your greatest challenge is learning how to handle stress, when tension in your personal and professional life can leave you feeling exhausted and nervous. Your best bet for maintaining optimal physical and emotional health is to practice deep breathing as well as stretching exercises. Low-impact aerobics can also help you build up endurance.

Use Venus transits through Capricorn or the other earth signs to correct bad habits. Jupiter transits promote a boost in optimism and self-esteem, giving you the confidence you need to make improvements in your lifestyle.

LUCKY LISTS: CAPRICORN

★　★　★　★

YOUR LUCKY NUMBERS
3 • 5 • 18 • 22

YOUR LUCKY COLORS
Magenta • Gray • Ice Blue • Flame

YOUR LUCKY STONES
Garnet • Black Obsidian • Carnelian • Marble

YOUR LUCKY DAY/MONTH
Saturday • January

YOUR LUCKY CITIES
Atlanta • Seattle • New York

YOUR LUCKY TRAVEL DESTINATIONS
India • Mexico • Bermuda

YOUR LUCKY PROFESSIONS
Dentist • Historian • Administrator

YOUR LUCKY HOBBIES
Collecting Antiques • Tennis • Musical Instruments

YOUR LUCKY ASSOCIATIONS (FRIENDS)
Taurus • Cancer • Virgo

MEDITATION
"Shift your focus from the familiar to the sublime."

AQUARIUS

★ ★ ★ ★

Air Sign
January 20 - February 18

YOUR SUN SIGN CHARACTERISTICS

AQUARIANS ARE INTELLIGENT, versatile individuals. You are known for your analytical skills and the ability to solve problems through interesting and original concepts.

Although often considered the "oddballs" of the zodiac, Aquarians are actually fascinating people who like to do things their own way. You have an intense, electrifying personality and possess the potential for achieving greatness on many levels. Whether in the world arena or simply your own backyard, you understand the importance of "making a difference."

You have a thirst for knowledge, though it isn't likely to be satisfied through conventional means. You're the opposite of conventional; you're an innovator, even a rebel. That often requires making waves, but you couldn't care less. You believe in speaking your mind, whatever the occasion or situation.

Uranus, the planet of chaotic change and revolution, rules your sign. Your altruistic but complex nature is a result of all that unfocused Uranian energy, and it is your challenge to find a way to channel it toward positive, progressive enlightenment.

You always seem to be in the midst of some change in your life, whether on the material or the ephemeral level. It is not your nature to stagnate. For you, learning is an abstract endeavor. Whenever you achieve a life goal, you're ready to move beyond it to challenge yourself on an even more demanding level.

When it comes to style, you set your own standards. Always eager to swim against the current, you probably prefer a very casual look. Even when you do dress to the nines, you manage to convey your own style in a very dramatic and uncompromising way. Because of your humanitarian concerns, you are likely to be against wearing fur or using any products that have been tested on animals.

YOUR LUCK: STRENGTHS AND WEAKNESSES

Aquarians are brilliant, talented, and unique individuals. You have a scintillating personality and great charisma. Even if you are not exceptionally good looking, you probably give the impression of being attractive because your personal aura is so arresting.

One of your finest traits is your humanitarianism. You truly care about people and are likely to be involved in some form of charity work. Aquarius embodies the spirit of volunteerism. You take your social responsibilities very seriously, realizing that it's not enough to simply talk about what should be done to make the world a better place. You are committed to being a part of the solution.

Although you are very aware of what trends are currently in fashion, you aren't the type to subscribe to something just because "everybody else is doing it." Individuality is the keynote to your nature, and it's something you manage to preserve throughout your life.

On the debit side, you can be extremely erratic at times, running hot and cold in your relationships. Sometimes you seem to put up a wall between yourself and the rest of the world. This can give others the impression that you're insensitive and unfeeling, even though you are very much the opposite.

YOUR LUCK IN: FAMILY

Your eccentric attitude extends to family life. You aren't the type who relegates people to roles, so you probably look upon your closest family members more as friends than relatives.

Although you take an interest in the lives of those you love, you never meddle in their lives or try to influence their decisions. Because you are open-minded and fair, you are probably regarded as the one person in your family upon whom everyone can rely for advice and sympathy.

Whenever Venus transits Aquarius (transit: a planet's passage through a sign), you may find yourself drawn into a closer, more emotionally satisfying relationship with a female member of the family. Jupiter transits in air signs may give you the opportunity to reconnect with family members who live far away. (See the Venus and Jupiter transit tables on pages 92–95.)

YOUR LUCK IN: RELATIONSHIPS

Aquarians have a reputation for surrounding themselves with a lot of friends. While it is true that you have a large circle of pals, you may actually have only a few very intimate friends. It isn't easy for you to get really close to people because you prefer to keep your emotions under wraps.

Your attitude toward love and romance can be equally quixotic. Even when you give your love to someone, a part of you yearns to be absolutely independent and free of emotional entanglements.

Venus cycles give you a chance to meet a new romantic partner or to cultivate additional friendships. When Jupiter passes through Aquarius, Gemini, or Libra, you have an instinct for connecting with people who bring joy and excitement into your life.

YOUR LUCK IN: MONEY

You have a natural talent for making money and a genuine flair for spending it. You aren't careless about money, but you do prefer a creative approach to handling your finances. That often means making decisions based on instinct rather than common sense.

Aquarians aren't particularly interested in making a lot of money. Sure, you like the nice things and useful gadgets it can buy, but you know better than to use it as a measure of your achievement. You can be incredibly generous with your resources and are always happy to help friends or family members in need.

You can expect financial success to intensify during Venus transits in Aquarius, Gemini, or Libra. Jupiter cycles are likely to bring exciting financial opportunities into your life, often through investments or legacies.

YOUR LUCK IN: HOME AND TRAVEL

Air-sign individuals have a natural affinity for travel. It is almost a way of life for you. You especially enjoy traveling with a group of close friends.

Your domestic life is often hectic. You enjoy filling your house with friends and associates for frequent parties and get-togethers. Other times, you need your private "space" and want the house to yourself, giving you the chance to read a good book without any interruptions.

You have interesting, eclectic tastes and generally handle your own decorating chores. One thing never changes: There are always plenty of books in every room!

When Venus transits your sign, you may be inspired to buy lovely new things or expensive antiques for your home. When Jupiter transits Aquarius or the other air signs, you can benefit from refinancing your home or having antiques appraised.

YOUR LUCK IN: HEALTH AND SELF-IMPROVEMENT

Aquarius governs the circulatory system, so you need plenty of regular exercise in order to keep healthy and fit. Unfortunately, many people of your sign have a sedentary lifestyle because they are more likely to channel this energy toward mental rather than physical activity.

Self-improvement is something very close to your heart. You are constantly looking for ways to make your life fuller. Many Aquarians endorse the New Age message. When you are ready to give up bad habits, such as eating too much red meat, it becomes a crusade for you.

Use Venus transits in the air signs to get more exercise, cut back on high-calorie foods, and find other ways to empower yourself. Look to Jupiter cycles for increased energy and optimism.

LUCKY LISTS: AQUARIUS

★ ★ ★ ★

YOUR LUCKY NUMBERS
8 • 11 • 26 • 33

YOUR LUCKY COLORS
Indigo • French Blue • Orchid • Rose

YOUR LUCKY STONES
Aquamarine • Black Pearl • Bloodstone • Malachite

YOUR LUCKY DAY/MONTH
Saturday • February

YOUR LUCKY CITIES
Dallas • New Orleans • Indianapolis

YOUR LUCKY TRAVEL DESTINATIONS
Russia • Sweden • Israel

YOUR LUCKY PROFESSIONS
Computer Analyst • Graphic Artist • Nutritionist

YOUR LUCKY HOBBIES
The Internet • Aerobics • New Age Studies

YOUR LUCKY ASSOCIATIONS (FRIENDS)
Gemini • Leo • Libra

MEDITATION
"What you see in others is only a reflection of yourself."

PISCES

★ ★ ★ ★

Water Sign

February 19 - March 20

YOUR SUN SIGN CHARACTERISTICS

Pisceans are imaginative individuals who appreciate the spiritual aspect of life. You are known for your generous spirit and the ability to make others feel good about themselves.

One of your best traits is the ability to accept people on their own terms. You don't expect others to conform to your standards, and you're very understanding when a loved one's opinions or lifestyle choices conflict with your own.

Pisceans have amazing artistic talents. You have a great understanding of and love for music, poetry, and/or photography. Whether professionally or as a hobby, you will find some way to incorporate these interests into your day-to-day life.

With Neptune as your ruling planet, you have a natural ability for healing that may draw you to the caring professions in medicine or therapy. No matter how satisfactory your life may be, you will always look for a way in which you can help others. You believe in trying to make the world better "one person at a time."

Although you believe in working hard and take pride in your achievements, you aren't particularly goal-oriented. You believe that life is a journey, and everything you learn along the way is an important lesson. "Life knowledge" and experience rather than book learning is something you value very much. At some time in your life, you may seek to withdraw temporarily from the world in order to give priority to a more spiritual existence.

When it comes to appearance, you aren't wedded to the idea that looking great equals feeling great. For you, it's far more important to feel comfortable with your "look." You don't like to come on strong, and you often "dress down" in order to appear less intimidating. You are particularly fond of accessories, especially pieces of jewelry that have strong sentimental value.

YOUR LUCK: STRENGTHS AND WEAKNESSES

You have an emotional and spiritual depth unequaled by any other sign. Pisceans who are in tune with their own feelings are the most enlightened people on the planet.

Your love for people and animals is one of the things that makes you so kind in every aspect of your life. You have absolutely no interest in succeeding at the expense of others. To you, if something is "meant to be," it will happen—without you sacrificing your principles. Although you value the good things that life has to offer, you can be happy with modest material possessions.

One of the drawbacks to your nature is an inability to solve your own problems because you are so busy trying to solve the problems of others. You sacrifice your own needs too easily in order to support your loved ones.

Because you don't know the meaning of the word "ego," you often allow yourself to be a follower, even though you have the moral and ethical authority to lead. When you aren't feeling particularly good about yourself, it is easy for you to become disinterested and undirected, frittering away your talents and inspiration instead of using them to their full potential.

YOUR LUCK IN: FAMILY

You are intensely involved in all aspects of family life. Because of your natural sensitivity and need to care for others, you develop deep and committed relationships with close family members. While it can be very hard for you to see children leave home for college or career opportunities, you also experience great joy and satisfaction from the achievements of those you love.

It is often common for the people of your sign to maintain close relationships with grown siblings, who have probably become more like good friends than family to you throughout the years.

Venus transits (transit: a planet's passage through a sign) bring a spirit of renewed harmony between family members. Jupiter's passage through Pisces, Cancer, or Scorpio may herald the arrival of a new addition to the family, or a successful period in the life of someone close to you. (See the Venus and Jupiter transit tables on pages 92–95.)

YOUR LUCK IN: RELATIONSHIPS

This is a complex area of life for you, since you are easily drawn into the concerns of your friends due to your kind and generous personality. You have a wide circle of pals and believe that no one can have too many friends.

Even though you may not seem to be a leader, you provide an extraordinary example for friends who flock to you for advice. The fact that you are such a good listener is only one indication of that quality.

Pisceans are very romantic people who never seem to lose the need to be loved. You don't like being without a sweetheart, and you only feel truly fulfilled if you have a loving mate or partner by your side.

Venus transits are periods when you can find yourself making a new friend or even falling in love! Jupiter cycles generally coincide with good news in the realm of personal relationships.

YOUR LUCK IN: MONEY

The typical Piscean is the sort of individual who will give away a cherished possession because a friend admires it. This doesn't mean that you don't understand the value of money; you simply place a higher price on other things.

When you are in the mood to spend money, you usually spend it on exquisite things—clothes, jewelry, paintings. Your artistic nature gives you a great love of beautiful things. Having them around you is more important to you than piling up money in the bank.

When it comes to making financial decisions, you may prefer to leave it to a professional. You don't like taking responsibility for financial matters, particularly if family resources are involved.

When Venus transits your sign, you can depend on small but unexpected financial gains to come your way. Jupiter's transit in Pisces, Cancer, or Scorpio is likely to increase your earnings by a sizable amount.

YOUR LUCK IN: HOME AND TRAVEL

You revel in your home life, seeing it as an atmosphere of harmony where you can relax and be yourself. Surrounded by the people and the things you love, you feel safe, as if nothing bad can happen to you.

Although travel may represent little more than a pleasant recreation for you, Pisceans often find themselves having to travel on a regular basis, usually for business purposes, at some point in life. When you take a vacation, you prefer to travel with a loved one or friend. Making a trip alone takes all the fun out of the experience for you.

When Venus transits the water signs, you may find yourself enjoying a group excursion or romantic trip for two. Jupiter's passage often accords with a prolonged visit to a foreign locale, or visits to you from friends who live abroad.

YOUR LUCK IN: HEALTH AND SELF-IMPROVEMENT

As a sensitive person, emotional matters have a big impact on your physical health. Stress, worry over a loved one, or just the blues can cause you to feel nervous and run-down. More than any other sign, you can benefit from taking herbal supplements that will relax and sustain you.

You have a great appreciation for mystical or New Age disciplines that involve mind/body wellness. Doing yoga and meditation on a regular basis can really add to your sense of physical, spiritual, and emotional well-being.

During Venus transits, you'll often feel exceptionally good about yourself. When Jupiter moves through the water signs, you have the positive energy you need to begin a whole new era of health consciousness.

LUCKY LISTS: PISCES

★ ★ ★ ★

YOUR LUCKY NUMBERS
2 • 4 • 10 • 20

YOUR LUCKY COLORS
Violet • Aqua • Sandalwood • Mint

YOUR LUCKY STONES
Amethyst • Coral • Smokey Quartz • Sapphire

YOUR LUCKY DAY/MONTH
Monday • March

YOUR LUCKY CITIES
Phoenix • Atlantic City • Minneapolis

YOUR LUCKY TRAVEL DESTINATIONS
Finland • Portugal • Argentina

YOUR LUCKY PROFESSIONS
Artist • Photographer • Psychiatrist

YOUR LUCKY HOBBIES
Flower Arranging • Dancing • Keeping Pets

YOUR LUCKY ASSOCIATIONS (FRIENDS)
Cancer • Virgo • Scorpio

MEDITATION
"The old and familiar are only that; pursue what
challenges and inspires."

VENUS TRANSIT TABLE

★ ★ ★ ★

Expect good luck when Venus transits your sign.

VENUS TRANSITS LEO:
July 13 - Aug. 5, 2000
Aug. 26 - Sept. 19, 2001
June 14 - July 9, 2002
July 28 - Aug. 21, 2003
Sept. 6 - Oct. 2, 2004
June 28 - July 21, 2005
Aug. 12 - Sept. 5, 2006
June 5 - July 13, 2007
July 12 - Aug. 4, 2008
Aug. 26 - Sept. 19, 2009
June 14 - July 9, 2010
July 28 - Aug. 20, 2011

VENUS TRANSITS VIRGO:
Aug. 6 - Aug. 29, 2000
Sept. 20 - Oct. 14, 2001
July 10 - Aug. 8, 2002
Aug. 22 - Sept. 14, 2003
Oct. 3 - Oct. 27, 2004
July 22 - Aug. 15, 2005
Sept. 6 - Sept. 29, 2006
July 14 - Nov. 7, 2007
Aug. 5 - Aug. 29, 2008
Sept. 20 - Oct. 13, 2009
July 10 - Aug. 5, 2010
Aug. 21 - Sept. 13, 2011

VENUS TRANSITS LIBRA:
Aug. 30 - Sept. 23, 2000
Oct. 15 - Nov. 7, 2001
Aug. 9 - Sept. 6, 2002
Sept. 15 - Oct. 8, 2003

Oct. 28 - Nov. 21, 2004
Aug. 16 - Sept. 10, 2005
Sept. 30 - Oct. 23, 2006
Nov. 8 - Dec. 4, 2007
Aug. 30 - Sept. 22, 2008
Oct. 14 - Nov. 6, 2009
Aug. 6 - Sept. 8, 2010
Sept. 14 - Oct. 8, 2011

VENUS TRANSITS SCORPIO:
Sept. 24 - Oct. 18, 2000
Nov. 8 - Dec. 1, 2001
Sept. 7, 2002 - Jan. 6, 2003
Oct. 9 - Nov. 1, 2003
Nov. 22 - Dec. 15, 2004
Sept. 11 - Oct. 6, 2005
Oct. 24 - Nov. 16, 2006
Dec. 5 - Dec. 29, 2007
Sept. 23 - Oct. 17, 2008
Nov. 7 - Nov. 30, 2009
Sept. 9, 2010 - Jan. 6, 2011
Oct. 9 - Nov. 1, 2011

VENUS TRANSITS SAGITTARIUS:
Oct. 19 - Nov. 11, 2000
Dec. 2 - Dec. 25, 2001
Jan. 7 - Feb. 3, 2003
Nov. 2 - Nov. 25, 2003
Dec. 16, 2004 - Jan. 8, 2005

Oct. 7 - Nov. 4, 2005
Nov. 17 - Dec. 10, 2006
Dec. 30, 2007 - Jan. 23, 2008
Oct. 18 - Nov. 11, 2008
Dec. 1 - Dec. 24, 2009
Jan. 7 - Feb. 3, 2011
Nov. 2 - Nov. 25, 2011

VENUS TRANSITS CAPRICORN:
Nov. 12 - Dec. 7, 2000
Dec. 26, 2001 - Jan. 17, 2002
Feb. 4 - March 1, 2003
Nov. 26 - Dec. 20, 2003
Jan. 9 - Feb. 1, 2005
Nov. 5 - Dec. 14, 2005
Dec. 11, 2006 - Jan. 2, 2007
Jan. 24 - Feb. 16, 2008
Nov. 12 - Dec. 6, 2008
Dec. 25, 2009 - Jan. 17, 2010
Feb. 4 - Feb. 28, 2011
Nov. 26 - Dec. 19, 2011

VENUS TRANSITS AQUARIUS:
Dec. 8, 2000 - Jan. 2, 2001
Jan. 18 - Feb. 10, 2002
March 2 - March 26, 2003
Dec. 21, 2003 - Jan. 13, 2004
Feb. 2 - Feb. 25, 2005
Dec. 15, 2005 - April 4, 2006

Jan. 3 - Jan. 26, 2007
Feb. 17 - March 11, 2008
Dec. 7, 2008 - Jan. 2, 2009
Jan. 18 - Feb. 10, 2010
March 1 - March 26, 2011

VENUS TRANSITS PISCES:
Jan. 3 - Feb. 1, 2001
Feb. 11 - March 6, 2002
March 27 - April 20, 2003
Jan. 14 - Feb. 7, 2004
Feb. 26 - March 21, 2005
April 5 - May 2, 2006
Jan. 27 - Feb. 20, 2007
March 12 - April 5, 2008
Jan. 3 - Feb. 1, 2009
Feb. 11 - March 6, 2010
March 27 - April 19, 2011

VENUS TRANSITS ARIES:
Feb. 2 - June 5, 2001
March 7 - March 31, 2002
April 21 - May 15, 2003
Feb. 8 - March 4, 2004
March 22 - April 14, 2005
May 3 - May 28, 2006
Feb. 21 - March 16, 2007
April 6 - April 29, 2008
Feb. 2 - June 5, 2009
March 7 - March 30, 2010
April 20 - May 14, 2011

VENUS TRANSITS TAURUS:
June 6 - July 4, 2001
April 1 - April 24, 2002
May 16 - June 8, 2003

March 5 - April 2, 2004
April 15 - May 8, 2005
May 29 - June 22, 2006
March 17 - April 10, 2007
April 30 - May 23, 2008
June 6 - July 4, 2009
March 31 - April 24, 2010
May 15 - June 8, 2011

VENUS TRANSITS GEMINI:
July 5 - July 31, 2001
April 25 - May 19, 2002
June 9 - July 3, 2003
April 3 - Aug. 6, 2004
May 9 - June 2, 2005
June 23 - July 17, 2006
April 11 - May 7, 2007

May 24 - June 17, 2008
July 5 - July 30, 2009
April 25 - May 18, 2010
June 9 - July 2, 2011

VENUS TRANSITS CANCER:
Aug. 1 - Aug. 25, 2001
May 20 - June 13, 2002
July 4 - July 27, 2003
Aug. 7 - Sept. 5, 2004
June 3 - June 27, 2005
July 18 - Aug. 11, 2006
May 8 - June 4, 2007
June 18 - July 11, 2008
July 31 - Aug. 25, 2009
May 19 - June 13, 2010
July 3 - July 27, 2011

JUPITER TRANSIT TABLE

★ ★ ★ ★

Expect good luck when Jupiter transits your sign.

JUPITER TRANSITS GEMINI:	June 30, 2000 - July 11, 2001
JUPITER TRANSITS CANCER:	July 12, 2001 - July 31, 2002
JUPITER TRANSITS LEO:	August 1, 2002 - August 26, 2003
JUPITER TRANSITS VIRGO:	August 27, 2003 - September 23, 2004
JUPITER TRANSITS LIBRA:	September 24, 2004 - October 24, 2005
JUPITER TRANSITS SCORPIO:	October 25, 2005 - November 22, 2006

JUPITER TRANSITS SAGITTARIUS:	November 23, 2006 - December 17, 2007
JUPITER TRANSITS CAPRICORN:	December 18, 2007 - January 4, 2009
JUPITER TRANSITS AQUARIUS:	January 5, 2009 - January 16, 2010
JUPITER TRANSITS PISCES:	January 17, 2010 - June 5, 2010 and September 7, 2010 - January 21, 2011
JUPITER TRANSITS ARIES:	June 6, 2010 - September 8, 2010 and January 22, 2011 - June 3, 2011
JUPITER TRANSITS TAURUS:	June 4, 2011 - June 10, 2012

JUPITER RETROGRADE TABLE

★ ★ ★ ★

These are periods when your luck levels off.

IN GEMINI:	September 29, 2000 - January 25, 2001
IN CANCER:	November 2, 2001 - March 1, 2002
IN LEO:	December 4, 2002 - April 3, 2003
IN VIRGO:	January 3, 2004 - May 4, 2004
IN LIBRA:	February 1, 2005 - June 5, 2005
IN SCORPIO:	March 4, 2006 - July 6, 2006
IN SAGITTARIUS:	April 5, 2007 - August 6, 2007
IN CAPRICORN:	May 9, 2008 - September 7, 2008
IN AQUARIUS:	June 15, 2009 - October 12, 2009
In PISCES:	September 8, 2010 - November 18, 2010
IN ARIES:	July 23, 2010 - September 8, 2010
IN TAURUS:	August 30, 2011 - December 25, 2011

BIRTHDAYS

★ ★ ★ ★

_____

_____

_____

_____

_____

_____

_____

_____

_____

_____

_____

_____

_____

_____